Dear Pete and the Smith Family, story!
Hope you enjoy Lizzie's story!
Thanks, Laurie, for helping us on
our Underground Railroad Experience.
It was fun — making history come alive!
The purpose of my book is on p. 33
where you see a *. (Hi, Connie!) :)
Love,
Mrs. Stives

The Door in the Floor

An Underground Railroad Adventure

JOAN TRINDLE STIVER

PICTURES BY KAREN GRUNTMAN

authorHOUSE®

AuthorHouse™
1663 Liberty Drive, Suite 200
Bloomington, IN 47403
www.authorhouse.com
Phone: 1-800-839-8640

First published by AuthorHouse 2/28/2008

ISBN: 978-1-4343-2953-0 (e)
ISBN: 978-1-4343-2952-3 (sc)

Library of Congress Control Number: 2008901457

Printed in the United States of America
Bloomington, Indiana

This book is printed on acid-free paper.

DEDICATION

This book is dedicated
to my precious grandchildren:
Kaitlin, Noah, Jared, Jamie, Andrew, Ashley,
and Levi.

It is also dedicated to Judy Miller and Suezell
Adams,
great friends and co-teachers at
Orchard View Elementary School.
Thanks for all the fun times!!!

J.S.

To D.D.G., with love, K.S.G.

ACKNOWLEDGEMENTS

I would like to thank the following people for their support and encouragement:

Suezell Adams, Ron Adams, Irvin Beck, Frank Fisher, Morgan and Betsy Forney, Karen Gruntman, Galen Kauffmann, Marcia Kindy, Brett and Kristin Martin, Judy Miller, Cathy Morgan, Kathy Meyer Reimer, Greg Stiver, Rich and Kirsten Stiver, Donna Stokes – Lucas, Terry Trimmer, Dorothy Trindle, and especially my high school sweetheart, my husband, Jim Stiver, who has been by my side encouraging me for 43 years.

A NOTE FROM THE AUTHOR:

When I was in the fourth grade during the fifties, our family vacationed in the south. My dad, mom, brother, and I were walking down a city sidewalk when a black man walked toward us. The black man stepped off the sidewalk down into the gutter and bowed to my dad, a white man. I remember seeing the top of his bald head. I looked up to my mom and started to ask "why". Mom gave me a quick "Be quiet, I'll tell you later" look. I was confused and I couldn't understand. In this story Lizzie Blue feels the same confusion.

CHAPTER 1

K.S. Grumblon
©07

Dark thunderclouds rolled in from the west as Lizzie was helping her Mama quickly take down laundry from the line. Lizzie noticed Mama anxiously looking around, not in the direction of the approaching storm, but over toward the woods to the south of their log cabin. The air was heavy and not one leaf was moving.

"Mama, what are you looking at?"

"Nothing, Lizzie. Quick, get the sheets folded and into the basket before the rain comes. At least this storm should break the heat. It sure is unsettled around here."

Lizzie Blue's birthdays were always hot, but this one, July 15, 1858, seemed hotter and more humid than ever. Lizzie was ten years old that day, but chores always came first at their northern Indiana farm. She knew her birthday would be full of work just like every other day, but she was looking forward to a nice present at supper.

Mama and Lizzie ran up the wooden step and across the front porch as a crack of thunder shook Lizzie's insides. Her two little sisters, five-year-old Amy and three-year-old Nettie, were playing with homemade dolls on the living room floor. The rain pelting on the roof made so much noise the two little girls started crying. Mama and Lizzie sat on the floor and held them. Mama always comforted her girls with her soft, sweet singing.

They calmed down just as Papa bolted through the back door. "I wasn't planning on taking a bath today," Papa laughed. The sight of Papa dripping all over the kitchen floor was so funny it made all three sisters laugh.

CHAPTER 2

Amy and Nettie were too little to help with chores. Almost all of Lizzie's days were full of taking care of them, feeding the chickens, gathering the eggs, and helping Mama with cooking and laundry.

Lizzie's papa, Abner Blue, had built a nice log cabin just north of Goshen. Lizzie loved the fireplace in the living room. It was made of rocks that Mama, Papa, and Lizzie had gathered from the fields out in back two years ago when Papa built the cabin. Papa always joked about all the rocks in his fields. He chuckled, "My fields grow rocks instead of corn!" The fireplace made long, cold winter nights warm and cozy, but they sure didn't need a fire that day.

Even though it was very hot, Mama fired up the stove so she could bake a little cake for Lizzie's birthday. After everyone was finished with supper and the special birthday dessert, Lizzie's bright eyes twinkled in anticipation at her mama. Mrs. Blue reached in a drawer, pulled out an old torn book, and handed it to her oldest daughter.

Lizzie was disappointed. The book was falling apart. Some pages were gone, and someone had tied string in two places to hold the pages together. Lizzie complained, "Why can't I have a new book or a toy for my birthday?"

Mama and Papa's faces fell. They looked so sad. Lizzie pouted as she slowly left the table. She put her book in her bedroom to look at later.

After the dishes were washed and the kitchen cleaned up, Lizzie put clean, white sheets on her bed. The sheets smelled like fresh air.

Lizzie shared a big bed with her sisters. They slept crossways on the bed. Lizzie slept in the middle with the two little sisters one on each side of her. Their bedroom was on one side of the living room and Mama and Papa's bedroom was on the other side. The little kitchen was behind the living room.

As Lizzie was getting ready to go to bed that night, she noticed something strange that Mama did. Mama lit the oil lamp that sat on a little table in front of the living room window. They never kept the lamps burning after they went to bed. Lizzie thought that was strange but she didn't ask any questions.

Her sisters were already asleep when Lizzie crawled in between them that night. Amy and Nettie usually took naps, but the storm had kept them awake that afternoon. The two little sisters were in a deep sleep, but Lizzie was so hot and unsettled she couldn't sleep. She forced her eyes to close and they just popped open. She closed them again and they popped open again.

After what seemed like a long time, she heard a quiet knock on the front door. She could hear Papa walk across the wooden living room floor to the door. He whispered, "Who is it?"

Someone on the front porch quietly said, "A friend with friends." Papa opened the door.

Lizzie had to see who was at the door. She snuck out of bed and tiptoed over to her bedroom door which was open a few inches. Standing in her dark room she peeked through the crack. Her eyes grew wide at what she saw.

Chapter 3

There were six black people coming in the
cabin, a mama, a papa, and four children.
Lizzie recognized the man who brought them
to the front door. He was Mr. Johnson, Papa's friend from church. A few weeks ago
Lizzie heard Papa, Mr. Johnson and some
other men at church talking about slavery

and how wrong it is, and how some people have to run from the south to search for freedom.

Before Mr. Johnson left, Lizzie heard him tell Papa about a group of men out to catch these people and take them back south to their owners. Papa said, "Hurry, hurry, get in here." He closed and locked the front door. He hurried over to the stone fireplace and leaned down in front of it to pull back the rug. Under the rug was a trap door cut in the floor. The Blue family used this tiny room under the living room to store potatoes, apples, and onions.

He said, "Get down here quickly. There's a ladder. Be careful!" As they were going down into this little space under the living room, Mama handed each one a piece of her homemade bread, a piece of cheese, and an apple. They really appreciated the food because they hadn't eaten all day.

Five of them got down in that hole, but there wasn't room for the last one. She was a girl a little younger than Lizzie. Papa smoothed out the rug over the door in the floor and started to look around for a place to hide the girl. He looked quickly around the living room and at the kitchen. Then he looked at the girls' bedroom door.

CHAPTER 4

Lizzie knew she'd better hurry back to bed or she'd be in trouble. When Mama and Papa put them to bed, they weren't allowed to get up until morning. She quickly closed her eyes and pretended to be asleep.

Papa, with a very scared little girl following him, came in by the bed and whispered, "Lizzie, Lizzie, wake up. We need your help."

Lizzie rubbed the pretend sleep out of her eyes and whispered, "Papa, how can I help you?"

"You have to help us hide this family. They're trying to work their way north to Vandalia, Michigan for their freedom. Why don't you girls hide in the closet?"

Not many people had closets when Lizzie was a girl because people didn't have many clothes. Usually just a few hooks on the wall would be enough to hang up clothes, but the three Blue girls were lucky. Papa had built a small closet when he built the cabin. It was a tiny room where the girls could hang their dresses and also wash up in private.

The two girls quickly sat down on the hard wooden floor and closed the door almost all the way.

CHAPTER 5

Lizzie's heart was beating fast. She didn't know what to say. Finally she said, "My name is Lizzie."

The girl said, "My name is Effie Mae."

Lizzie added, "My birthday's today. I'm ten years old."

Surprised, Effie Mae said, "My birthday's today too. My mama told me this morning I'm eight years old today."

Lizzie was happy to have something to talk about so she asked her what she got for her birthday. Effie Mae said her mama had given her some wild flowers she had picked early that morning. The wilted flowers were still in Effie Mae's pocket. Lizzie told Effie Mae she got an old book.

Effie Mae was just about finished eating the food Mama had given her when Lizzie asked if she would like some of her birthday cake. A big smile told Lizzie the answer was "yes". "I'll be right back, Effie Mae."

She tiptoed out of the closet and out of her room across the living room floor to the kitchen. She took her birthday cake down off the shelf, cut a piece, and put it on a saucer along with two forks. She quietly snuck back into her room and into the closet. Lizzie whispered, "Effie Mae, I'll share a piece of my birthday cake with you."

Effie Mae took one bite and rolled the sweetness around on her tongue. Lizzie could tell she loved it. "You can have it all, Effie Mae. I already had a piece after supper."

Chapter 6

Effie Mae and Lizzie talked and giggled, told stories and giggled, quietly sang songs and giggled some more. She told Lizzie what it was like to live on a plantation down south. She had to be out in the fields every day and pick cotton right along side her mama. She didn't even get to go to school.

Effie Mae shared, "I always got tired working in the fields, but we sang songs. I liked that because it made the days go faster. Many times Mama said they can take lots of things away from us, but they can't take our singing voices."

"When you're traveling to the north how do you know which way to go, Effie Mae?"

"Well, most of the time a man takes us from one place to another. We've had so many different men leading us to the north that I've lost track how many. But sometimes at night we follow the drinking gourd."

With a puzzled look on her face Lizzie asked, "What's a 'drinking gourd'?"

Effie Mae laughed, "You don't know what the drinking gourd is up in the sky at night?" Effie Mae explained to Lizzie they had to follow the drinking gourd stars to escape to the north. Papa told Lizzie later that they call that group of stars the Big Dipper and the outer stars always point to the North Star.

Lizzie asked, "Effie Mae, how can you tell which way is north at night when it's cloudy?"

She told Lizzie, "My papa taught me that moss grows on the north side of trees. So when we walk through a dark woods, we feel the moss on the tree trunks and we know which way to go."

"Effie Mae, Your mama and papa are really brave to leave their family and friends without even knowing where they're going to end up. They are very courageous."

"I know they are, Lizzie. My mama and papa have to trust strangers to help us. If we get caught they might split us up, and I may never see my family again."

"I never thought about it before but I guess my family already has freedom, Effie Mae. Why do you and your family have to run away to get freedom? I mean, it's such a long way and it's so dangerous."

"I guess it's because our skin is dark, Lizzie." Several seconds of silence passed as Lizzie was trying to understand.

"That just doesn't make sense, Effie Mae." Lizzie's new friend slowly hung her head. Lizzie thought she was going to cry.

"I know," said Effie Mae.

* * * *

The two girls had fun that night. Effie Mae was the first girlfriend Lizzie ever had. The closest family lived almost two miles down the road, and they had only boys in their family.

The rain had almost stopped. Effie Mae was in the middle of telling Lizzie about her two brothers and how cute her baby sister was when they heard a very loud knock on the front door. Lizzie was afraid her sisters would wake up.

Chapter 7

"ABNER, ABNER BLUE! DO YOU HAVE ANY RUNAWAY SLAVES HIDDEN IN THERE?" ABNER, OPEN UP!"

Lizzie couldn't see Papa but she heard him walk quickly to the front door. He opened it and said, "Good evening, Gentlemen." The girls could hear several men on the front porch, but only one man spoke.

"We heard there are slaves around here tonight. We saw fresh footprints in the mud a ways back. You know it's against the law to hide them, don't you?"

Papa said, "Yes, but I haven't seen any. If I do, I'll be sure and let you know."

Four men stepped into the living room. One went out to the kitchen to search. Another man stood on top of the rug in front of the fireplace. Lizzie could hear the floor creak under the man's feet. Another started for the girls' room.

In the dark closet two quiet girls clung to each other in fear. Their hearts were pounding so hard they were afraid the men would hear them. Papa whispered, "My daughters are asleep in there."

"Well, we're going to check in your barn and chicken coop just to make sure."

"Go ahead," said Papa.

One of the most important things Mama and Papa always taught their daughters was to tell the truth! They were never allowed to tell lies. Now Lizzie heard her papa telling a lie. She couldn't understand it. She was confused.

The girls held hands as they huddled together on the closet floor. Their throats were dry and the palms of their hands were sweaty. They finally heard the men ride away on their horses.

Soon Papa came in the room and opened the closet door. "Lizzie, it's time for them to go."

Lizzie cried, "No, Papa, no. Effie Mae is my friend. I'm just getting to know her."

He interrupted, "No, Honey, they have to work their way up to Owen Coffin's house in Bristol in the next couple days and then on up to Michigan. It's time."

Lizzie gave her new friend a hug and cried, "Effie Mae, I want to give you something to re-member me." She went over to her chest of drawers which she shared with her sisters. It had three drawers and each one of the girls had a drawer. Lizzie's drawer was the top one. She quietly pulled it open and reached to the back. She felt what she wanted and slowly took it out.

It was a pretty pin with shiny jewels on it. Lizzie could hardly talk because she was crying. "Effie Mae, I want you to have this pin. My grandma gave it to me two years ago for my eighth birthday. I want you to have it now for your eighth birthday."

She said, "No, I can't take that. I've never had anything like that."

Lizzie put it in Effie Mae's hand and closed her fingers around it. "Yes, Effie Mae, you take this and you'll always remember the fun we had tonight.

"Lizzie, I want to give you something too. Please take my wildflowers."

"Oh, thank you, Effie Mae. I can press them in the book I got for my birthday present."

Effie Mae added, "Our birthday presents will be together forever!" The girls hugged each other one more time through their tears.

"Effie Mae, maybe some day we can be friends again."

Effie Mae agreed, "Maybe . . . some day."

CHAPTER 8

Morning greeted Lizzie with bright sunshine, a deep blue sky, and clean crisp air. The heavy humidity was gone. She followed the smell of bacon frying into the kitchen where Mama and Papa were having breakfast.

As she sat down at the table Lizzie apologized to her parents for acting so selfish and ungrateful when Mama gave her the book for her birthday present.

"You grew up quite a bit yesterday on your tenth birthday, didn't you, Lizzie?"

"Yes, Papa. I realize now why you didn't have much money to spend on my birthday present. All the extra money went to help feed Effie Mae's family."

Papa added, "Not only do we give freedom seekers food, but also clothes, and your mama gives them some of her quilts she makes so they'll have something to keep them warm on chilly nights."

Surprised, Lizzie asked, "You mean you've done this before?"

Her parents smiled. "Yes, Dear, for about two years now – as long as we've been living here. We use our storage cellar to hide people on their way north."

Mama set a plate with a fried egg and two slices of bacon on it and a glass of milk on the table in front of Lizzie.

Mama went on to explain that the burning oil lamp at night was a sign. She said, "When they see the light in the window, they know this is a safe house, a place they can hide."

Papa took another sip of his coffee. "If a man knocks on our door and says, 'a friend with friends,' then I know he's a conductor. Mr. Johnson is one of the conductors on the Underground Railroad."

Lizzie ate another bite of fried egg. Confused, Lizzie said, "Papa, we don't have a railroad around here."

Papa smiled lovingly at his daughter. "Lizzie, the Underground Railroad isn't a real railroad at all. It's made up of many roads that slaves use to escape to the north. Some people call it 'the freedom trail'. It's called 'underground' because they travel at night in secrecy. We are called 'abolitionists' because we want to abolish or get rid of slavery. Lizzie, you must understand how important it is that you speak to no one about this."

"Yes, Papa."

Mama and Papa hid and took care of people looking for freedom many times after that. Lizzie loved to help them, but she had a nagging question inside her that never went away – Why do people have to risk their lives for freedom?

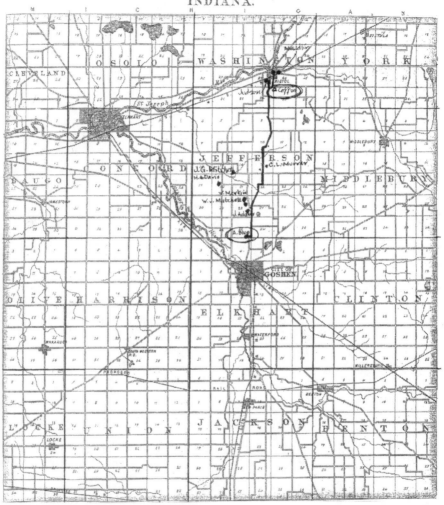

1874
SECTIONAL MAP OF
ELKHART COUNTY
INDIANA.

This map of Elkhart County in Indiana is the earliest map that could be found. It was given to the author by the Elkhart County Historical Museum in Bristol, Indiana. The little dots represent the known Underground Railroad safe houses in Elkhart County before the Civil War. Abner Blue's and Own Coffin's farms are circled.

Dear Boys and Girls, This story is fiction, but it is based on several facts. One of the many places in our country the freedom seekers came to the north was Goshen and Bristol in Elkhart County, Indiana. Some went on to Canada, but some settled in Vandalia or Calvin Center in Cass County, Michigan. Several descendants of slaves still live there. Abner Blue was a real man who lived north of Goshen on what is now State Road 15 and he did help some people seeking their freedom. One of the safe houses in Bristol was owned by Owen Coffin. He was a relative of Levi Coffin who is known as "the president of the Underground Railroad". Levi Coffin's house north of Richmond, Indiana, is a registered National Historic Landmark. The rest of the characters in this story are fictitious. The Fugitive Slave Act of 1850 said that it was against the law for people to hide or help the runaways. Some slaves were caught in northern Indiana and returned to their masters in the south. The Emancipation Proclamation effective January 1, 1863, said that all persons held as slaves shall be free, but many problems remained. Prejudice and discrimination still exist today. Lizzie's question at the end of the story has never really been answered.

Dear Parents and Teachers, You may want to use these discussion questions with your children after finishing the book. My hope is that you will use this story to help you as you begin to teach your children about prejudice and discrimination.

1. In the story Lizzie said she heard her papa telling a lie to the men who were looking for Effie Mae's family. Can you think of situations in which it is okay to tell a lie?
2. In what ways did Lizzie change from the beginning of the story to the end?
3. Think of a time when you were selfish or ungrateful. How did you change or grow from the situation?
4. What does freedom mean to you? Is it so important that people risk their lives for it?
5. Think of a time when you left your home, friends, and everything that was familiar to you for a while. Compare and contrast your situation with Effie Mae's situation.
6. Can you create a sequel to this story? Pretend that Lizzie and Effie Mae meet again in about twenty years after this story ends. What objects in the story would help the two main characters recognize each other? Think about the setting, the characters, and the plot. You may want to add some new characters besides Lizzie and Effie Mae. Then write down your ideas or your plan before you start writing your story.

About the Author:

A retired elementary school teacher, JOAN STIVER lives in Middlebury, Indiana. She calls Elkhart, Indiana her hometown but she has lived in North Dakota and Michigan as well. She and her husband have four children and seven grandchildren. Joan graduated from Purdue University with a B.A. and an M.S. in Education. She has enjoyed teaching preschool, and second and fourth grades. Now Joan enjoys volunteering as the music teacher at her church daycare and as a tutor at the same school where she taught. She and her husband love to travel and visit their grandchildren in three different states.

Visit her website at
www.joanstiver.com.

ABOUT THE ILLUSTRATOR:

KAREN GRUNTMAN was raised in a small town in southern Michigan and at an early age discovered the joys of drawing and coloring. Many happy hours were spent tracing elaborate composite scenes using Walt Disney coloring book characters.   Learning to read was very difficult for Karen and the illustrations on the book's pages were what beckoned her to explore within the pages. To this day many books have been chosen for her library because of the illustrations.

Karen studied art at Central Michigan University, and taught elementary art for 20 years, teaching children from Kindergarten through 5th grade. This is the fifth book she has illustrated. She and her husband live in northern Indiana. When she is not up in her studio working on various art projects, she enjoys photography, travel, and especially spending time with the family.

This is a rarely shared secret -- Karen loves mice and hides them in her illustrations. Get out the magnifying glass and have a look.

14 of them

Printed in the United States
109585LV00002B/1-165/P